Teachers/Maestros

By JoAnn Early Macken

Reading consultant: Susan Nations, M.Ed., author/literacy coach/consultant

Gareth Stevens
Publishing

Please visit our Web site www.garethstevens.com. For a free color catalog of all our high-quality books, call toll free 1-800-542-2595 or fax 1-877-542-2596.

Cataloging Data

Macken, JoAnn Early, 1953-
    Teachers/Maestros by JoAnn Early Macken.
       p. cm. — (People in my community/Mi comunidad)
    Summary: Photographs and simple text introduce the work of the teacher, who helps children learn how to read, write, and count. Bilingual edition.
    Includes bibliographical references and index.
    ISBN: 978-1-4339-3766-8 (pbk.)
    ISBN: 978-1-4339-3767-5 (6-pack)
    ISBN: 978-1-4339-3765-1 (library binding)
    1. Teachers—Juvenile literature. 2. Teaching—Vocational guidance—Juvenile literature.
[1. Teachers. 2. Occupations. 3. Spanish-language materials] I. Title. II. Series.

New edition published 2010 by
Gareth Stevens Publishing
111 East 14th Street, Suite 349
New York, NY 10003

New text and images this edition copyright © 2010 Gareth Stevens Publishing

Original edition published 2003 by Weekly Reader® Books
An imprint of Gareth Stevens Publishing
Original edition text and images copyright © 2003 Gareth Stevens Publishing

Art direction: Haley Harasymiw, Tammy Gruenewald
Page layout: Michael Flynn, Katherine A. Goedheer
Editorial direction: Kerri O'Donnell, Diane Laska Swanke
Spanish translation: Eduardo Alamán

Photo credits: Cover, pp. 1, 9, 13, 17 © Shutterstock.com; pp. 5, 7, 11, 15, 19, 21 by Gregg Andersen.

Printed in the United States of America

CPSIA compliance information: Batch #WW10GS: For further information contact Gareth Stevens, New York, New York at 1-800-542-2595.

Table of Contents

Contenido

Boldface words appear in the glossary/
Las palabras en **negrita** aparecen en el glosario

A Teacher's Busy Day

Teachers help students learn in school. Students can learn the **alphabet**! Students also learn to read and write.

- -

Un día muy ocupado

Los maestros ayudan a los alumnos a aprender en la escuela. ¡Los alumnos pueden aprender el **abecedario**! También pueden aprender a leer y a escribir.

Sometimes teachers use games to teach students new things.

A veces, los maestros usan juegos para enseñarles cosas nuevas a los alumnos.

Subtraction signal words:

left
more
fewer
less
difference

Addition signal words:

in a
alto

Can
Did
Is

Who
What
Where
When
Why
How
Are
Was
Will
Do May
Could

Teachers read books with students. Teachers might use a computer to help students learn.

Los maestros leen libros a sus alumnos. A veces, usan computadoras para enseñarles nuevas lecciones.

computer/
computadora

Teachers answer questions.
Teachers ask questions, too.
Do you know the answer?
Raise your hand!

Los maestros responden
preguntas. Los maestros
también hacen preguntas.
¿Sabes la respuesta? ¡Alza
una mano!

Some teachers teach many **subjects**, like math, reading, and writing. Some teachers teach just one subject, like science, music, or art.

Algunos maestros enseñan varias **materias**, como matemática, lectura y escritura. Otros, sólo enseñan una materia. Ésta puede ser música, ciencia o arte.

A Field Trip!

Sometimes a teacher takes students on a **field trip**. They might visit a zoo or a **museum** to learn new things.

¡De paseo!

A veces, el maestro lleva a los alumnos **de paseo**. El paseo puede ser al zoológico o a un **museo** para aprender cosas nuevas.

Teachers Hard at Work

Teachers work at school and at home. At home, they correct papers and tests. They plan what they will teach.

Trabajando duro

Los maestros trabajan en casa y en la escuela. En casa revisan las tareas y los exámenes. Además planean sus clases.

Teachers meet with adults to tell them how their children are doing at school.

Los maestros se reúnen con los padres de sus alumnos para decirles cómo van en la escuela.

It's fun to share what you learn in school!

¡Es muy divertido compartir lo que aprendes en la escuela!

Glossary/Glosario

alphabet: the letters that make up all the words we say and write

field trip: a visit made by a teacher and students to learn new things

museum: a place where interesting objects are shown

subject: an area of learning, such as art, math, or science

- -

abecedario (el) Las letras que usamos para leer o escribir

materia (la) Un área de aprendizaje, como arte, matemática o ciencia

museo (el) Un lugar donde se muestran objetos interesantes

paseo (el) Una visita que hace el maestro con los alumnos para aprender algo

For More Information/Más información

Books/Libros

Campbell, Frank, *¿Quién está en la escuela? (Who's at School?)* Real Readers en español. New York. Rosen Classroom, 2006

Leake, Diyan. *Los maestros (Teachers).* Personas de la comunidad / People in the Community (Collection) Spanish Edition. Heinemann Library, 2009

Web Sites/Páginas en Internet

Bureau of Labor Statistics Career Information
http://www.bls.gov/k12/help01.htm

Index/Índice

About the Author

JoAnn Early Macken is the author of children's poetry, two rhyming picture books, *Cats on Judy* and *Sing-Along Song,* and various other nonfiction series. She teaches children to write poetry and received the Barbara Juster Esbensen 2000 Poetry Teaching Award. JoAnn is a graduate of the MFA in Writing for Children Program at Vermont College. She lives in Wisconsin with her husband and their two sons.

- -

Información sobre la autora

JoAnn Early Macken es autora de libros de poesía infantil, dos libros ilustrados, *Cats on Judy* y *Sing-Along Song,* y varias series de libros informativos. JoAnn recibió en 2000 el Premio Barbara Juster Esbensen por su trabajo como maestra de poesía infantil. JoAnn vive en Wisconsin con su esposo y sus dos hijos.